# INDIAN LODGE-FIRE STORIES

War Eagle in his lodge

# INDIAN LODGE-FIRE STORIES

*By*
Frank B. Linderman
*[Co-skee-see-co-cot]*

*Foreword by*
Carl Schreier

*Illustrated by*
Charles M. Russell

HOMESTEAD PUBLISHING
Moose, Wyoming

Cover illustration of "Clears Up" by Winold Reiss.

ISBN 0-943972-39-6

*Library of Congress Cataloging-in-Publication Data*

Linderman, Frank Bird, 1869-1938
    Indian lodge-fire stories / by Frank B. Linderman ; foreword by Carl Schreier ; illustrated by Charles M. Russell.
        p.        cm.
    Originally published: New York : C. Scribners's sons, c1918.
    ISBN 0-943972-39-6 (alk. paper)
    1. Siksika Indians—Folklore. 2. Ojibwa Indians—Folklore. 3. Cree Indians—Folklore. 4. Legends—North America. I. Title.
E98.F6L68    1998
398.2'089'973—dc21                                                        98-12660
                                                                                      CIP

Printed in the United States of America on recycled, acid free paper.

Published by
HOMESTEAD PUBLISHING
Box 193 • Moose, Wyoming 83012

# CONTENTS

FOREWORD ..................................................................... 7

INTRODUCTION ............................................................. 9

WHY THE CHIPMUNK'S BACK IS STRIPED ..................... 13

HOW THE DUCKS GOT THEIR FINE FEATHERS ........... 25

WHY OUR SIGHT FAILS WITH AGE .............................. 31

WHY THE KINGFISHER ALWAYS WEARS A
    WAR-BONNET ........................................................ 39

WHY THE CURLEW'S BILL IS LONG AND
    CROOKED .............................................................. 47

WHY BLACKFEET NEVER KILL MICE ........................... 53

OLD-MAN STEALS THE SUN'S LEGGINGS ..................... 61

WHY THE NIGHT-HAWK'S WINGS ARE
    BEAUTIFUL ............................................................. 71

THE FIRE-LEGGINGS ..................................................... 79

WHY INDIANS WHIP THE BUFFALO-BERRIES
    FROM THE BUSHES ................................................ 85

WHY THE BIRCH-TREE WEARS THE SLASHES
    IN ITS BARK .......................................................... 91

# Foreword

Only occasionally does a writer emerge who, out of respect, cherishes his subject. Frank Bird Linderman was such a writer. He was the predecessor of great naturalist-writers like Walter McClintock, George Bird Grinnell and James Willard Shultz—who in their own right left an indelible record of the northern Plains Indian at a time of an indifferent government, and before their life changed and vanished forever.

Today these naturalists romantic and poetic lives seem touched with intrinsic values of altruism, especially compared to our own empty but complex turn-of-the-twentieth-century lives. For us there is a perplexing question. Did these early chroniclers living among tribal Americans, slightly beyond a stone-age culture, discover mysteries and secrets to harmony and a balance with nature?

In 1885 Linderman sought wilderness solace at an early age of sixteen and a half. With his parents blessing he left the comforts of his Ohio home to trap, trade, homestead and live among Indians in a faraway wilderness—known as Montana. His boyish dream turned to reality as he immersed himself in the customs, language and life of the Flathead, Kootenai, Kalispel, (now collectively called the Salish Confederacy) Blackfeet, Crows, Crees, and Chippewas in an area around Glacier National Park along the front range of the Rocky Mountains. To improve his communicative skills among this diverse group he mastered sign language—the universal form of communication among tribes. For this he was even given the name "Mah-paht-sa-mot-tsasa", meaning *Great Sign Talker*, by the Crows.

The first Native American he befriended upon arriving to his new adopted land was Red-Horn, a well-known Flathead. Even though, Linderman later recounted, he did not know a Flathead from a Kootenai. Red-Horn made great efforts at their first meeting to tell him through sign language that he was a Flathead, not a Kootenai—who were considered hostile. Linderman learned to "talk" through him to discover Flathead cultural and social customs during their lifelong friendship.

Linderman's boyish dream of a wilderness life lasted six years until he met and married Minnie Jane Johns, a courageous and independent woman who became his source of encouragement. After their marriage new responsibilities lead Linderman to accept employment as an assayer in Butte, Montana; a publisher of the *Sheridan Chinook;* a representative of the state legislature in Helena; and from 1906-1909, Assistant Secretary of State. For the following eight years he was a successful insurance agent with the whole state of Montana as his territory. Meanwhile the Lindermans also raised three daughters—Wilda, Verne and Norma.

During his stint as a politician his greatest accomplishment was the establishment of Rocky Boy Reservation. This reservation, however, was achieved under great political strife, but it established a home for Crees and Chippewas, who were left out of the system and were known as the "landless Indians".

By 1917 the Lindermans had saved enough money to build their dream home on the shore of Flathead Lake in northwestern Montana where he embarked on a long awaited career as a writer. The tamarack log home on Goose Bay as his daughter Verne described it was located on, "a square bay on Flathead Lake. A wooded slope came down like sheltering arms from the hills behind the house. There was not a neighbor on either side; only virgin timber back of us, and, before us, the lake, rimmed on the far shore by the blue mountains, ten or twelve miles away." It was a haven to visiting family, writers, artists and friends, including Charley Russell, the cowboy artist, who illustrated many of Frank's books.

At Goose Bay Frank wrote about what he cherished most—the life of the Plains Indian before the inception of European descendants. His works are based on his early wilderness years while living among the reservation Blackfeet where he established a lifelong association with tribesmen. Even though Linderman had first-hand account of Indian life during the late 1880s he felt that it was "far too late to study the Indian." Even so Linderman was only one of a handful of "white interpreters" to have taken the initiative to do so.

What he desired to do was accurately portray Indian life, their folklore and their religion. Especially of their God, or Manitou, and the creator, Napa or Oldman, who in his fallible way created their world; and in many ways answered and simplified life's perplexing questions. These stories capture the oral storytellers legends that have been passed down generation after generation.

Linderman, for one, may have come close to discovering what we all have pursued—the quintessential answer to the mysteries and secrets to harmony and a balance with nature.

*Carl Schreier*
*Moose, Wyoming*
*Summer 1998*

# INTRODUCTION

It was the moon when leaves were falling, for Napa had finished painting them for their dance with the North wind. Just over the ragged mountain range the big moon hung in an almost starless sky, and in shadowy outline every peak lay upon the plain like a giant pattern. Slowly, the light spread and as slowly the shadows stole away until the October moon looked down on the great Indian camp – a hundred lodges, each as perfect in design as the tusks of a young silver-tip, and all looking ghostly white in the still of the autumn night.

Back from the camp, keeping within the ever-moving shadows, a buffalo-wolf skulked to a hill overlooking the scene, where he stopped to look and listen, his body silhouetted against the sky. A dog howled occasionally, and the weird sound of a tom-tom accompanying the voice of a singer in the Indian village reached the wolf's ears, but caused him no alarm; for not until a great herd of ponies, under the eyes of the night-herder, drifted too close, did he steal away.

Near the center of the camp was the big painted lodge of War Eagle, the medicine-man, and inside had gathered his grandchildren, to whom he was telling the stories of the creation and of the strange doings of Napa, the creator. Being a friend of the old historian, I entered unhindered, and with the children listened until the hour grew late, and on the lodge-wall the dying fire made warning shadows dance.

*F.B.L.*

# Why the Chipmunk's Back is Striped

# Why the Chipmunk's Back is Striped

WHAT a splendid lodge it was, and how grand War Eagle looked leaning against his back-rest in the firelight! From the tripod that supported the back-rest were suspended his weapons and his medicine-bundle, each showing the wonderful skill of the maker. The quiver that held the arrows was combined with a case for the bow, and colored quills of the porcupine had been deftly used to make it a thing of beauty. All about the lodge hung the strangely painted linings, and the firelight added richness to both color and design. War Eagle's hair was white, for he had known many snows; but his eyes were keen and bright as a boy's, as he gazed in pride at his grandchildren across the lodge-fire. He was wise, and had been in many battles, for his was a warlike tribe. He knew all about the world and the people in it. He was deeply religious, and every Indian child loved him for his goodness and brave deeds.

About the fire were Little Buffalo Calf, a boy of eleven years; Eyes-in-the-Water, his sister, a girl of nine; fine Bow, a cousin of these, aged ten, and Bluebird, his sister, who was but eight years old.

Not a sound did the children make while the old

warrior filled his great pipe, and only the snapping of the lodge-fire broke the stillness. Solemnly, War Eagle lit the tobacco that had been mixed with the dried inner bark of the red willow, and for several minutes smoked in silence, while the children's eyes grew large with expectancy. Finally he spoke:

"Napa, *Old*-man, is very old indeed. He made this world, and all that is on it. He came out of the south, and traveled toward the north, making the birds and animals as he passed. He made the perfumes for the winds to carry about, and he even made the war-paint for the people to use. He was a busy worker, but a great liar and thief, as I shall show you after I have told you more about him. It was *Old*-man who taught the beaver all his cunning. It was *Old*-man who told the bear to go to sleep when the snow grew deep in winter, and it was he who made the curlew's bill so long and crooked, although it was not that way at first. *Old*-man used to live on this world with the animals and birds. There was no other man or woman then, and he was chief over all the animal-people and the bird-people. He could speak the language of the robin, knew the words of the bear, and understood the sign-talk of the beaver, too. He lived with the wolves, for they are the great hunters. Even today, we make the same sign for a smart man as we make for the wolf; so you see he taught them much while he lived with them. *Old*-man made a great many mistakes in making things, as I shall show you after a while; yet he worked until he had everything good. But he often made great mischief and taught many wicked things. These I shall tell you about some day. Everybody was afraid of *Old*-man and his tricks and lies – even the animal-people, before he made men and women. He used to visit the lodges of our people and make trouble long ago, but he got so wicked that Manitou grew angry at him, and one day in the month of roses, he built a lodge for *Old*-man and told him that he must stay in it forever. Of course he had to do that, and nobody knows where the lodge was built, nor in what country, but that is why we never see him as our grandfathers did, long, long ago.

"What I shall tell you now happened when the world was young. It was a fine summer day, and *Old*-man was traveling in the forest. He was going north and straight as an arrow – looking at nothing, hearing nothing. No one knows what he was after, to this day. The birds and forest-people spoke politely to him as he passed but he answered none of them. The Pine-squirrel, who is always trying to find out other people's business, asked him where he was going, but *Old*-man wouldn't tell him. The woodpecker hammered on a dead tree to make him look that way, but he wouldn't. The Elk-people and the Deer-people saw him pass, and all said that he must be up to some mischief or he would stop and talk a while. The pine-trees murmured, and the bushes whispered their greeting, but he kept his eyes straight ahead and went on traveling.

"The sun was low when *Old*-man heard a groan" (here War Eagle groaned to show the children how it sounded), "and turning about he saw a warrior lying bruised and bleeding near a spring of cold water. *Old*-man knelt beside the man and asked: 'Is there war in this country?'

"'Yes,' answered the man. 'This whole day long we have fought to kill a Person, but we have all been killed, I am afraid.'

"'That is strange,' said *Old*-man; how can one Person kill so many men? Who is this Person, tell me his name!' but the man didn't answer – he was dead. When *Old*-man saw that life had left the wounded man, he drank from the spring, and went on toward the north, but before long he heard a noise as of men fighting, and he stopped to look and listen. Finally he saw the bushes bend and sway near a creek that flowed through the forest. He crawled toward the spot, and peering through the brush saw a great Person near a pile of dead men, with his back against a pine-tree. The Person was full of arrows, and he was pulling them from his ugly body. Calmly the Person broke the shafts of the arrows, tossed them aside, and stopped the blood flow with a brush of his hairy hand. His head was large and fierce-looking, and his eyes were small and wicked. His great body was larger than that of a buffalo-bull and covered with scars of many battles.

"The Person was full of arrows, and he was pulling them
from his ugly body"

"*Old*-man went to the creek, and with his buffalo-horn cup brought some water to the Person, asking as he approached:

"'Who are you, Person? Tell me, so I can make you a fine present, for you are great in war.'

"'I am Bad Sickness,'" replied the Person. "'Tribes I have met remember me and always will, for their bravest warriors are afraid when I make war upon them. I come in the night or I visit their camps in daylight. It is always the same; they are frightened and I kill them easily.'

"'Ho!' said *Old*-man, 'tell me how to make Bad Sickness, for I often go to war myself.' He lied; for he was never in a battle in his life. The Person shook his ugly head and then *Old*-man said:

"'If you will tell me how to make Bad Sickness I will make you small and handsome. When you are big as you now are, it is very hard to make a living; but when you are small, little food will make you fat. Your living will be easy because I will make your food grow everywhere.'

"'Good,' said the Person, 'I will do it; you must kill the fawns of the deer and the calves of the elk when they first begin to live. When you have killed enough of them you must make a robe of their skins. Whenever you wear that robe and sing – "now you sicken, now you sicken," the sickness will come – that is all there is to it.'

20

"'Good,' said *Old*-man, 'now lie down to sleep and I will do as I promised.'

"The Person went to sleep and *Old*-man breathed upon him until he grew so tiny that he laughed to see how small he had made him. Then he took out his paint sack and striped the Person's back with black and yellow. It looked bright and handsome and he waked the Person, who was now a tiny animal with a bushy tail to make him pretty.

"'Now,' said *Old*-man, 'you are the Chipmunk, and must always wear those striped clothes. All of your children and their children must wear them, too.'

"After the Chipmunk had looked at himself, and thanked *Old*-man for his new clothes, he wanted to know how he could make his living, and *Old*-man told him what to eat, and said he must cache the pine-nuts when the leaves turned yellow, so he would not have to work in the winter time.

"'You are a cousin to the Pine-squirrel,' said *Old*-man, 'and you will hunt and hide as he does. You will be spry and your living will be easy to make if you do as I have told you.'

"He taught the Chipmunk his language and his signs, showed him where to live, and then left him, going on toward the north again. He kept looking for the cow-elk and doe-deer, and it was not long before he had killed enough of their young to make the robe as the Person told him, for they were plentiful before the white

21

man came to live on the world. He found a shady place near a creek, and there made the robe that would make Bad Sickness whenever he sang the queer song, but the robe was plain, and brown in color. He didn't like the looks of it. Suddenly he thought how nice the back of the Chipmunk looked after he had striped it with his paints. He got out his old paint sack and with the same colors made the robe look very much like the clothes of the Chipmunk. He was proud of the work, and liked the new robe better; but being lazy, he wanted to save himself work, so he sent the South-wind to tell all the doe-deer and the cow-elk to come to him. They came as soon as they received the message, for they were afraid of *Old*-man and always tried to please him. When they had all reached the place where *Old*-man was he said to them:

"'Do you see this robe?'

"'Yes, we see it,' they replied.

"'Well, I have made it from the skins of your children, and then painted it to look like the Chipmunk's back, for I like the looks of that Person's clothes. I shall need many more of these robes during my life; and every time I make one, I don't want to have to spend my time painting it; so from now on and forever your children shall be born in spotted clothes. I want it to be that way to save me work. On all the fawns there must be spots of white like this (here he pointed to the spots on Bad Sickness's robe) and on all of the elk-calves the

22

spots shall not be so white and shall be in rows and look rather yellow.' Again he showed them his robe, that they might see just what he wanted.

"'Remember,' he said, 'after this I don't want to see any of your children running about wearing plain clothing, because that would mean more painting for me. Now go away, and remember what I have said, lest I make you sick.'

"The cow-elk and the doe-deer were glad to know that their children's clothes would be beautiful, and they went away to their little ones who were hidden in the tall grass, where the wolves and mountain-lions would have a hard time finding them; for you know that in the tracks of the fawn there is no scent, and the wolf cannot trail him when he is alone. That is the way Manitou takes care of the weak, and all of the forest-people know about it, too.

"Now you know why the Chipmunk's back is striped, and why the fawn and elk-calf wear their pretty clothes.

"I hear the owls, and it is time for all young men who will some day be great warriors to go to bed, and for all young women to seek rest, lest beauty go away forever. Ho!"

# How the Ducks Got Their Fine Feathers

## How the Ducks Got Their Fine Feathers

ANOTHER night had come, and I made my way toward War Eagle's lodge. In the bright moonlight the dead leaves of the quaking-aspen fluttered down whenever the wind shook the trees; and over the village great flocks of ducks and geese and swan passed in a never-ending procession, calling to each other in strange tones as they sped away toward the waters that never freeze.

In the lodge War Eagle waited for his grandchildren, and when they had entered, happily, he laid aside his pipe and said:

"The Duck-people are traveling tonight just as they have done since the world was young. They are going away from winter because they cannot make a living when ice covers the rivers.

"You have seen the Duck-people often. You have noticed that they wear fine clothes but you do not know how they got them; so I will tell you tonight.

"It was in the fall when leaves are yellow that it happened, and long, long ago. The Duck-people had gathered to go away, just as they are doing now. The buck-deer was coming down from the high ridges to visit friends in the lowlands along the streams as they have always done. On a lake *Old*-man saw the Duck-people getting ready to go away, and at that time they all looked alike; that is, they all wore the same colored clothes. The loons and the geese and the ducks were there and playing in the sunlight. The loons were laughing loudly and the diving was fast and merry to see. On the hill where *Old*-man stood there was a great deal of moss, and he began to tear it from the ground and roll it into a great ball. When he had gathered all he needed he shouldered the load and started for the shore of the lake, staggering under the weight of the great burden. Finally the Duck-people saw him coming with his load of moss and began to swim away from the shore. "'Wait, my brothers!' he called, 'I have a big load here, and I am going to give you people a dance. Come and help me get things ready.'

"'Don't you do it,' said the gray goose to the others; 'that's *Old*-man and he is up to something bad, I am sure.'

"So the loon called to *Old*-man and said they wouldn't help him at all.

"Right near the water *Old*-man dropped his ball of moss and then cut twenty long poles. With the poles he built a lodge which he covered with the moss, leaving a doorway facing the lake. Inside the lodge he built a fire and when it grew bright he cried:

"'Say, brothers, why should you treat me this way when I am here to give you a big dance? Come into the lodge,' but they wouldn't do that. Finally *Old*-man began to sing a song in the duck-talk, and keep time with his drum. The Duck-people liked the music, and swam a little nearer to the shore, watching for trouble all the time, but *Old*-man sang so sweetly that pretty soon they waddled up to the lodge and went inside. The loon stopped near the door, for he believed that what the gray goose had said was true, and that *Old*-man was up to some mischief. The gray goose, too, was careful to stay close to the door but the ducks reached all about the fire. Politely, *Old*-man passed the pipe, and they all smoked with him because it is wrong not to smoke in a person's lodge if the pipe is offered, and the Duck-people knew that.

"'Well,' said *Old*-man, 'this is going to be the Blind-dance, but you will have to be painted first.

"'Brother Mallard, name the colors – tell how you want me to paint you.'

"'Well,' replied the mallard drake, 'paint my head green, and put a white circle around my throat, like a necklace. Besides that, I want a brown breast and yellow legs; but I don't want my wife painted that way.'

"*Old*-man painted him just as he asked, and his wife, too. Then the teal and the wood-duck (it took a long time to paint the wood-duck) and the spoonbill and the blue bill and the canvasback and the goose and the brant and the loon – all chose their paint. *Old*-man painted them all just as they wanted him to, and kept singing all the time. They looked very pretty in the

29

firelight, for it was night before the painting was done.

"'Now,' said *Old*-man, 'as this is the Blind-dance, when I beat upon my drum you must all shut your eyes tight and circle around the fire as I sing. Every one that peeks will have sore eyes forever.'

"Then the Duck-people shut their eyes and *Old*-man began to sing: 'Now you come, ducks, now you come – tum-tum, tum; tum-tum, tum.'

"Around the fire they came with their eyes still shut, and as fast as they reached *Old*-man, the rascal would seize them, and wring their necks. Ho! things were going fine for *Old*-man, but the loon peeked a little, and saw what was going on; several others heard the fluttering and opened their eyes, too. The loon cried out, 'He's killing us – let us fly,' and they did that. There was a great squawking and quacking and fluttering as the Duck-people escaped from the lodge. Ho! but *Old*-man was angry, and he kicked the back of the loon-duck, and that is why his feet turn from his body when he walks or tries to stand. Yes, that is why he is a cripple today.

"And all of the Duck-people that peeked that night at the dance still have sore eyes – just as *Old*-man told them they would have. Of course they hurt and smart no more but they stay red to pay for peeking, and always will. You have seen the mallard and the rest of the Duck-people. You can see that the colors *Old*-man painted so long ago are still bright and handsome, and they will stay that way forever and forever. Ho!"

# WHY OUR SIGHT FAILS WITH AGE

# Why Our Sight Fails With Age

CHICKADEE-DEE-DEE-DEE. Chicka-dee-dee-dee-dee.

"Oh, he almost came inside the lodge, grandfather!" cried Bluebird, as a chickadee flew to a bush near the door. "I like the chickadees. They are always so friendly and happy. I pretend they are laughing when they are in the willows and rosebushes. They do seem to be laughing, don't they, grandfather?"

"Yes," said War Eagle. "That is what *Old*-man thought one day long ago. It made trouble for us all, too – bad trouble that visits us if we live to be old."

"Tell us the story, grandfather!" cried Buffalo-Calf. "We will help grandmother gather dry wood if you will tell us about *Old*-man."

"That is good. I will tell you," said War Eagle. "It was in the forest where great trees grew, and where many bushes and vines covered the ground about them. *Old*-man was alone. He had seen no people since morning, and the Sun was already looking toward his lodge in the West. 'Listen,' he said; but he was only talking to himself. 'Listen.' He bent and placed his hand behind his ear, that he might hear better. Ha! somebody was laughing among the trees and bushes. It was not loud laughing, but the Person was having a good time all by himself, whoever it was.

"'That is funny – so much laughing,' said *Old*-man. 'I'll go and see who it is that laughs. I'd like to laugh, myself, if I could find something funny. I have looked, too, and there is nothing to laugh at.'

"He hurried toward the sound of laughing, making so much noise in his traveling that he could not hear the Person laugh. He stopped and listened. Ho! it was gone. The Person had moved. *Old*-man stood very still for a while, and then he heard the laughing again, but it was far away.

"'That is strange,' he said. 'That Person seems to find something that makes him happy wherever he goes. He was here and laughed, but I can see nothing to laugh at. Now he is over near that big tree and is laughing again. I must find that Person.'

"He hurried onward. He even ran; but twice the Person moved with his laugh before he came close to a small tree with thick leaves upon its branches.

"'Chickadee-dee-dee-dee. Chickadee-dee-dee-dee.' Ho! it was the Chickadee laughing.

"'What are you laughing at?' asked *Old*-man. 'I've traveled hard all this day and haven't seen a funny thing.'

"'That makes me laugh,' said the Chickadee. And he did laugh. 'Chickadee-dee-dee-dee!'

"'Are you laughing at me?' cried *Old*-man.

"'No. Oh, no – not exactly,' said the Chickadee. 'But if a Person cannot get along with himself, how can he laugh? Laugh is a prisoner with a cross person.'

"'What were you laughing at before I came?' asked *Old*-man.

"'Watch me,' said the Chickadee.

"Then he took out his eyes and tossed them away up among the branches. The Chickadee sat very still and waited for them to come down again. The eyes came straight back and landed plump! in their places, as if they had not been away. 'Chickadee-dee-dee-dee!' He was laughing again, and that made *Old*-man laugh too.

"'Ha, Ha, Ha! That *is* funny. Do it again.'

"'All right. Watch me,' said the Chickadee.

"Up went his eyes a second time, and down they came plump! into their places. And the Chickadee laughed again.

"'Ha-ha, ha! ha, ha, ha! That *is* funny. Show me how to do it, Chickadee,' said *Old*-man.

"'Oh, no – no,' said the Chickadee. 'You cannot do it. Your are too clumsy. You can do nothing well, and in trying you might get into trouble.'

"'Please, brother,' begged *Old*-man. 'Tell me the secret. I will be careful. I made you, and you should be good to me.'

"'Yes,' said the Chickadee, 'you made me, but you made a lot of enemies for me, too. I have more than anybody, and they are everywhere. No, this is my secret. You would blame me if you tried it and got into trouble.'

"'No, I will never blame you, brother. Tell me the secret and I will give you my necklace. See, it is very handsome.'

"The Chickadee looked at the necklace and became proud. He wanted to wear it. He thought it would make him more beautiful, so he said: 'All right, I'll tell you the secret. Then you must look out for yourself. I don't do this thing very often, myself, and I'm not clumsy as you are. You take out your eyes and throw them as high as you want them to go. They will always come straight back to their places if you do not move, nor laugh, nor even breathe while they are away. If you do any of these things, your eyes will be lost. Remember that. I have told you what not to do, and if you forget you will have to pay for it. That is all there is to the secret. Now give me that necklace.'

"*Old*-man took off his necklace and gave it to the Chickadee. Then he cried: 'Watch me.' He took out his eyes and tossed them far up among the trees. He stood still – did not laugh – did not move – did not even breathe. Plump! the eyes came back to their places as the Chickadee had said they would. *Old*-man laughed, and the Chickadee laughed with him.

"'Good-by, my brother. I shall have something to laugh at now,' said *Old*-man. And he went away in the forest.

"He tried the Chickadee's trick over and over, laughing each time, and each time tossing his eyes higher, until at last he grew careless. Ho! he moved his head. He laughed. He even breathed before his eyes came back. He was standing in a thickly timbered spot when he tossed his eyes upward. They were gone a long time. He was all ready to laugh, and couldn't wait. He heard something strike the ground near him. Then he was frightened. He was blind. He had no eyes. They had fallen on the ground among the dead leaves and dirt. Ho! *Old*-man was in trouble. Now he did not laugh. He cried. Yes, he cried. Oh ho! now he was sorry that he had met the Chickadee. He got down on his hands and knees and began to feel about for his eyes as one feels for things in the dark. Once he touched a snail and thought it was one of his eyes.

"Then at last he found his eyes in the dirt and leaves where they had fallen. He put them back in their places, but they hurt him because of the dirt that had clung to them while they were upon the ground. He never got over it. No. He could never see so well as he had before he did that foolish thing.

"Of course he made us all pay for his trouble. He always does. When he knew his eyes would never be so good as they were before he met the Chickadee that day, he said:

"'After this there shall come a time in the lives of old people when their eyes shall not be very useful.

They shall bother them before they die, as my eyes bother me.' It has been true from that day to this.

"The Chickadee and all his children wear *Old*-man's necklace since that day, and you have seen it about their necks, of course. The necklace is too heavy for a bird so small as the Chickadee, and its weight keeps him from flying very high in the air. He always stays near the ground in the bushes or small trees because of the heavy necklace that *Old*-man gave him that day in the forest. Ho!"

# Why the Kingfisher Always Wears a War-Bonnet

## WHY THE KINGFISHER ALWAYS
## WEARS A WAR-BONNET

AUTUMN nights on the upper Missouri river in
Montana are indescribably beautiful, and under
their spell imagination is a constant companion to him
who lives in wilderness, lending strange, weird echoes
to the voice of man or wolf, and unnatural shapes in
shadow to commonplace forms.

The moon had not yet climbed the distant mountain range to look down on the humbler lands when I
started for War Eagle's lodge; and dimming the stars in
its course, the milky way stretched across the jeweled
sky. "The wolf's trail," the Indians call this filmy streak
that foretells fair weather, and tonight it promised much,
for it seemed plainer and brighter than ever before.

"How – how!" greeted War Eagle, making the sign
for me to be seated near him, as I entered his lodge.
Then he passed me his pipe and together we smoked
until the children came.

Entering quietly, they seated themselves in exactly the same positions they had occupied on the
previous evenings, and patiently waited in silence.
Finally War Eagle laid the pipe away and said: "Ho!
Little Buffalo Calf, throw a big stick on the fire and

I will tell you why the Kingfisher wears a war-bonnet."

The boy did as he was bidden. The sparks jumped toward the smoke-hole and the blaze lighted up the lodge until it was bright as daytime, when War Eagle continued:

"You have often seen Kingfisher at his fishing along the rivers, I know; and you have heard him laugh in his queer way, for he laughs a good deal when he flies. That same laugh nearly cost him his life once, as you will see. I am sure none could see the Kingfisher without noticing his great head-dress, but not many know how he came by it because it happened so long ago that most men have forgotten.

"It was one day in the winter-time when *Old*-man and the Wolf were hunting. The snow covered the land and ice was on all of the rivers. It was so cold that *Old*-man wrapped his robe close about himself and his breath showed white in the air. Of course the Wolf was not cold; wolves never get cold as men do. Both *Old*-man and the Wolf were hungry for they had traveled far and had killed no meat. *Old*-man was complaining and grumbling, for his heart is not very good. It is never well to grumble when we are doing our best, because it will do no good and makes us weak in our hearts. When our hearts are weak our heads sicken and our strength goes away. Yes, it is bad to grumble.

"When the sun was getting low *Old*-man and the

Wolf came to a great river. On the ice that covered the water, they saw four fat Otters playing.

"'There is meat,' said the Wolf; 'wait here and I will try to catch one of those fellows.'

"'No! – No!' cried *Old*-man, 'do not run after the Otter on the ice, because there are air-holes in all ice that covers rivers, and you may fall in the water and die.' *Old*-man didn't care much if the Wolf did drown. He was afraid to be left alone and hungry in the snow – that was all.

"'Ho!' said the Wolf, 'I am swift of foot and my teeth are white and sharp. What chance has an Otter against me? Yes, I will go,' and he did.

"Away ran the Otters with the Wolf after them, while *Old*-man stood on the bank and shivered with fright and cold. Of course the Wolf was faster than the Otter, but he was running on the ice, remember, and slipping a good deal. Nearer and nearer ran the Wolf. In fact he was just about to seize an Otter, when SPLASH! – into an air-hole all the Otters went. Ho! the Wolf was going so fast he couldn't stop, and SWOW! into the air hole he went like a badger after mice, and the current carried him under the ice. The Otters knew that hole was there. That was their country and they were running to reach that same hole all the time, but the Wolf didn't know that.

"*Old*-man saw it all and began to cry and wail as women do. Ho! but he made a great fuss. He ran along the bank of the river, stumbling in the snowdrifts, and crying like a woman whose child is dead; but it was because he didn't want to be left in that country alone that he cried – not because he loved his brother, the Wolf. On and on he ran until he came to a place where the water was too swift to freeze, and there he waited and watched for the Wolf to come out from under the ice, crying and wailing and making an awful noise, for a man.

"Well – right there is where the thing happened. You see, Kingfisher can't fish through the ice and he knows it, too; so he always finds places like the one *Old*-man found. He was there that day, sitting on the limb of a birch-tree, watching for fishes, and when *Old*-man came near to Kingfisher's tree, crying like an old woman, it tickled the Fisher so much that he laughed that queer, chattering laugh.

"*Old*-man heard him and – Ho! but he was angry. He looked about to see who was laughing at him and that made Kingfisher laugh again, longer and louder than before. This time *Old*-man saw him and SWOW! he threw his war-club at Kingfisher; tried to kill the bird for laughing. Kingfisher ducked so quickly that *Old*-man's club just grazed the feathers on his head, making them stand up straight.

"'There,' said *Old*-man, 'I'll teach you to laugh at me when I'm sad. Your feathers are standing up on the top of your head now and they will stay that way, too.

As long as you live you must wear a head-dress, to pay for your laughing, and all your children must do the same.

"This was long, long ago, but the Kingfishers have not forgotten, and they all wear war-bonnets, and always will as long as there are Kingfishers.

"Now I will say good night, and when the sun sleeps again I will tell you why the curlew's bill is so long and crooked. Ho!"

# Why the Curlew's Bill is Long
## and Crooked

## WHY THE CURLEW'S BILL IS LONG AND CROOKED

WHEN we reached War Eagle's lodge we stopped near the door for the old fellow was singing – singing some old, sad song of younger days and keeping time with his tom-tom. Somehow the music made me sad and not until it had ceased, did we enter.

"How! How!" – he greeted us, with no trace of the sadness in his voice that I detected in his song.

"You have come here tonight to learn why the Curlew's bill is so long and crooked. I will tell you, as I promised, but first I must smoke."

In silence we waited until the pipe was laid aside, then War Eagle began:

"By this time you know that *Old*-man was not always wise, even if he did make the world, and all that is on it. He often got into trouble, but something always happened to get him out of it. What I shall tell you now will show you that it is not well to try to do things just because others do them. They may be right for others, and wrong for us, but *Old*-man didn't understand that, you see.

"One day he saw some mice playing and went near to watch them. It was springtime, and the frost was just coming out of the ground. A big flat rock was sticking out of a bank near a creek, and the sun had melted the frost from the earth about it, loosening it, so that it was about to fall. The Chief-Mouse would sing a song, while all the other mice danced, and then the chief would cry 'now!' and all the mice would run past the big rock. On the other side, the Chief-Mouse would sing again, and then say 'now!' – back they would come – right under the dangerous rock. Sometimes little bits of dirt would crumble and fall near the rock, as though warning the mice that the rock was going to fall, but they paid no attention to the warning, and kept at their playing. Finally *Old*-man said:

"'Say, Chief-Mouse, I want to try that. I want to play that game. I am a good runner.

"He wasn't, you know, but he thought he could run. That is often where we make great mistakes – when we try to do things we were not intended to do.

"'No – no!' cried the Chief-Mouse, as *Old*-man prepared to make the race past the rock. 'No! – No! – you will shake the ground. You are too heavy, and the rock may fall and kill you. My people are light of foot and fast. We are having a good time, but if you should try to do as we are doing you might get hurt, and that would spoil our fun.'

"'Ho!' said *Old*-man, 'stand back! I'll show you what a runner I am.'

"He ran like a grizzly bear and shook the ground

50

with his weight. SWOW! – came the great rock on top
of *Old*-man and held him fast in the mud. My! how he
screamed and called for aid. All the Mice-people ran away
to find help. It was a long time before the Mice-people
found anybody, but they finally found the Coyote, and
told him what had happened. Coyote didn't like *Old*-
man very much, but he said he would go and see what
he could do, and he did. The Mice-people showed him
the way, and when they all reached the spot – there
was *Old*-man deep in the mud, with the big rock on his
back. He was angry and was saying things people should
not say, for they do no good and make the mind wicked.

"Coyote, said: 'Keep still, you big baby. Quit kick-
ing about so. You are splashing mud in my eyes. How
can I see with my eyes full of mud? Tell me that. I am
going to try to help you out of your trouble.' He tried
but *Old*-man insulted Coyote, and called him a name
that is not good, so the Coyote said, 'Well, stay there,'
and went away.

"Again *Old*-man began to call for helpers, and the
Curlew, who was flying over, saw the trouble, and came
down to the ground to help. In those days Curlew had a
short, stubby bill, and he thought that he could break the
rock by pecking it. He pecked and pecked away without
making any headway, till *Old*-man grew angry at him, as
he did at the Coyote. The harder the Curlew worked, the
worse *Old*-man scolded him. *Old*-man lost his temper al-
together, you see, which is a bad thing to do for we lose

our friends with it, often. Temper is like a bad dog about a lodge – no friend will come to see us when he is about.

"Curlew did his best but finally said: 'I'll go and try to find somebody else to help you. I guess I am too small and weak. I shall come back to you.' He was standing close to *Old*-man when he spoke, and *Old*-man reached out and grabbed the Curlew by the bill. Curlew began to scream – oh, my – oh, my – oh, my – as you still hear them in the air when it is morning. *Old*-man hung onto the bill and finally pulled it out long and slim, and bent it downward, as it is today. Then he let go and laughed at the Curlew.

"'You are a queer-looking bird now. That is a homely bill, but you shall always wear it and so shall all of your children, as long as there are Curlews in the world.'

"I have forgotten who it was that got *Old*-man out of his trouble, but it seems to me it was the bear. Anyhow he did get out somehow, and lived to make trouble, until Manitou grew tired of him.

"There are good things that *Old*-man did and to-morrow night, if you will come early, I will tell you how *Old*-man made the world over after the water made its war on the land, scaring all the animal-people and the bird-people. I will also tell you how he made the first man and the first woman and who they were. But now the grouse is fast asleep; nobody is stirring, but those who were made to see in the dark, like the owl and the wolf. Ho!"

# WHY BLACKFEET NEVER KILL MICE

# Why Blackfeet Never Kill Mice

MUSKRAT and his grandmother were gathering wood for the camp the next morning, when they came to an old buffalo skull. The plains were dotted with these relics of the chase, for already the hide-hunting white man had played havoc with the great herds of buffalo. This skull was in a grove of cottonwood trees near the river, and as they approached two Mice scampered into it to hide. Muskrat, in great glee, secured a stick and was about to turn the skull over and kill the Mice, when his grandmother said: "No, our people never kill Mice. Your grandfather will tell you why if you ask him. The Mice-people are our friends and we treat them as such. Even small people can be good friends, you know – remember that."

All the day the boy wondered why the Mice people should not be harmed; and just at dark he came for me to accompany him to War Eagle's lodge. On the way he told me what his grandmother had said, and that he intended to ask for the reason, as soon as we arrived. We found the other children already there, and almost before we had seated ourselves, Muskrat asked:

"Grandfather, why must we never kill the Mice-people? Grandmother said that you knew."

"Yes," replied War Eagle, "I do know and you must know. Therefore I shall tell you all tonight why the Mice-people must be let alone and allowed to do as they please, for we owe them much; much more than we can ever pay. Yes – they are great people, as you will see.

"It happened long, long ago, when there were few men and women on the world. *Old*-man was chief of all then, and the animal people and the bird-people were greater than our people, because we had not been on earth long and were not wise.

"There was much quarreling among the animals and the birds. You see the Bear wanted to be chief, under *Old*-man, and so did the Beaver. Almost every night they would have a council and quarrel over it. Beside the Bear and Beaver, there were other animals, and also birds, that thought they had the right to be chief. They couldn't agree and the quarreling grew worse as time went on. Some said the greatest thief should be chosen. Others thought the wisest one should be the leader; while some said the swiftest traveler was the one they wanted. So it went on and on until they were most all enemies instead of friends, and you could hear them quarreling almost every night, until *Old*-man came along that way.

"He heard about the trouble. I forget who told him, but I think it was the Rabbit. Anyhow he visited the council where the quarreling was going on and listened to what each one had to say. It took until almost daylight, too. He listened to it all – every bit. When they had finished talking and the quarreling commenced as usual, he said, 'stop!' and they did stop.

"Then he said to them: 'I will settle this thing right here and right now, so that there will be no more rows over it, forever.'

"He opened his paint sack and took from it a small, polished bone. This he held up in the firelight, so that they might all see it, and he said:

"'This will settle the quarrel. You all see this bone in my right hand, don't you?'

"'Yes,' they replied.

"'Well, now you watch the bone and my hands, too, for they are quick and cunning.'

"*Old*-man began to sing the gambling song and to slip the bone from one hand to the other so rapidly and smoothly that they were all puzzled. Finally he stopped singing and held out his hands – both shut tight, and both with their backs up.

"'Which of my hands holds the bone now?' he asked them.

"Some said it was in the right hand and others claimed that it was the left hand that held it. *Old*-man asked the Bear to name the hand that held the bone, and the Bear did; but when *Old*-man opened that hand it was empty – the bone was not there. Then everybody laughed at the Bear. *Old*-man smiled a little and began to sing and again pass the bone.

"'Beaver, you are smart; name the hand that holds the bone this time.'

"The Beaver said: 'It's in your right hand. I saw you put it there.'

" *Old*-man opened that hand right before the Beaver's eyes, but the bone wasn't there, and again everybody laughed – especially the Bear.

"'Now, you see,' said *Old*-man, 'that this is not so easy as it looks, but I am going to teach you all to play the game; and when you have all learned it, you must play it until you find out who is the cleverest at the playing. Whoever that is, he shall be chief under me, forever.'

"Some were awkward and said they didn't care much who was chief, but most all of them learned to play pretty well. First the Bear and the Beaver tried it, but the Beaver beat the Bear easily and held the bone for ever so long. Finally the Buffalo beat the Beaver and started to play with the Mouse. Of course the Mouse had small hands and was quicker than the Buffalo – quicker to see the bone. The Buffalo tried hard for he didn't want the Mouse to be chief but it didn't do him any good; for the Mouse won in the end.

"It was a fair game and the Mouse was chief under the agreement. He looked quite small among the rest but he walked right out to the center of the council and said:

"Yes–the Mice-people always make their nests in the heads
of the dead Buffalo-people, ever since that night"

"'Listen, brothers – what is mine to keep is mine to give away. I am too small to be your chief and I know it. I am not warlike. I want to live in peace with my wife and family. I know nothing of war. I get my living easily. I don't like to have enemies. I am going to give my right to be chief to the man that *Old*-man has made like himself.'

"That settled it. That made the man chief forever, and that is why he is greater than the animals and the birds. That is why we never kill the Mice-people.

"You saw the Mice run into the buffalo skull, of course. There is where they have lived and brought up their families ever since the night the Mouse beat the Buffalo playing the bone game. Yes – the Mice-people always make their nests in the heads of the dead Buffalo-people, ever since that night.

"Our people play the same game, even today. See," and War Eagle took from his paint sack a small, polished bone. Then he sang just as *Old*-man did so long ago. He let the children try to guess the hand that held the bone, as the animal-people did that fateful night; but, like the animals, they always guessed wrong. Laughingly War Eagle said:

"Now go to your beds and come to see me tomorrow night. Ho!"

OLD-MAN STEALS THE SUN'S LEGGINGS

## OLD-MAN STEALS THE SUN'S LEGGINGS

FIRELIGHT – what a charm it adds to storytelling. How its moods seem to keep pace with situations pictured by the oracle, offering shadows when dread is abroad, and light when a pleasing climax is reached; for interest undoubtedly tends the blaze, while sympathy contributes or withholds fuel, according to its dictates.

The lodge was alight when I approached and I could hear the children singing in a happy mood, but upon entering, the singing ceased and embarrassed smiles on the young faces greeted me; nor could I coax a continuation of the song.

Seated beside War Eagle was a very old Indian whose name was Red Robe, and as soon as I was seated, the host explained that he was an honored guest; that he was a Sioux and a friend of long standing. Then War Eagle lighted the pipe, passing it to the distinguished friend, who in turn passed it to me, after first offering it to the Sun, the father, and the Earth, the mother of all that is.

In a lodge of the Blackfeet, the pipe must never be passed across the doorway. To do so would insult the host and bring bad luck to all who assembled. Therefore if there be a large number of guests ranged about

63

the lodge, the pipe is passed first to the left from guest to guest until it reaches the door, when it goes back, unsmoked, to the host, to be refilled ere it is passed to those on his right hand.

Briefly War Eagle explained my presence to Red Robe and said:

"Once the Moon made the Sun a pair of leggings. Such beautiful work had never been seen before. They were worked with the colored quills of the Porcupine and were covered with strange signs, which none but the Sun and the Moon could read. No man ever saw such leggings as they were, and it took the Moon many snows to make them. Yes, they were wonderful leggings and the Sun always wore them on fine days, for they were bright to look upon.

"Every night when the Sun went to sleep in his lodge away in the west, he used the leggings for a pillow, because there was a thief in the world, even then. That thief and rascal was *Old*-man, and of course the Sun knew all about him. That is why he always put his fine leggings under his head when he slept. When he worked, he almost always wore them, as I have told you, so that there was no danger of losing them in the daytime; but the Sun was careful of his leggings when night came and he slept.

"You wouldn't think that a person would be so foolish as to steal from the Sun, but one night *Old*-man — who is the only person who ever knew just where the

Sun's lodge was – crept near enough to look in, and saw the leggings under the Sun's head.

"We have all traveled a great deal, but no man ever found the Sun's lodge. No man knows in what country it is. Of course, we know it is located somewhere west of here, for we see him going that way every afternoon, but *Old*-man knew everything – except that he could not fool the Sun.

"Yes – *Old*-man looked into the lodge of the Sun and saw the leggings there – saw the Sun, too, and the Sun was asleep. He made up his mind that he would steal the leggings so he crept through the door of the lodge. There was no one at home but the Sun, for the Moon has work to do at night just as the children, the Stars, do, so he thought he could slip the leggings from under the sleeper's head and get away.

"He got down on his hands and knees to walk like the Bear-people and crept into the lodge, but in the black darkness he put his knee upon a dry stick near the Sun's bed. The stick snapped under his weight with so great a noise that the Sun turned over and snorted, scaring *Old*-man so badly that he couldn't move for a minute. His heart was not strong – wickedness makes every heart weaker – and after making sure that the Sun had not seen him, he crept silently out of the lodge and ran away.

"On the top of a hill *Old*-man stopped to look and listen, but all was still; so he sat down and thought.

"'I'll get them tomorrow night when he sleeps again,' he said to himself. 'I need those leggings myself, and I'm going to get them, because they will make me handsome as the Sun.'

"He watched the Moon come home to camp and saw the Sun go to work, but he did not go very far away because he wanted to be near the lodge when night came again.

"It was not long to wait, for all the *Old*-man had to do was to make mischief, and only those who have work to do measure time. He was close to the lodge when the Moon came out, and there he waited until the Sun went inside. From the bushes *Old*-man saw the Sun take off his leggings and his eyes glittered with greed as he saw their owner fold them and put them under his head as he had always done. Then he waited a while before creeping closer. Little by little, the old rascal crawled toward the lodge, till finally his head was inside the door. Then he waited a long, long time, even after the Sun was snoring.

"The strange noises of the night bothered him, for he knew he was doing wrong, and when a Loon cried on a lake nearby, he shivered as with cold, but finally crept to the sleeper's side. Cautiously his fingers felt about the precious leggings until he knew just how they could best be removed without waking the Sun. His breath was short and his heart was beating as a wardrum beats, in the black dark of the lodge. Sweat –

cold sweat, that great fear always brings to the weak-hearted – was dripping from his body, and once he thought that he would wait for another night, but greed whispered again, and listening to its voice, he stole the leggings from under the Sun's head.

"Carefully he crept out of the lodge, looking over his shoulder as he went through the door. Then he ran away as fast as he could go. Over hills and valleys, across rivers and creeks, toward the east. He wasted much breath laughing at his smartness as he ran, and soon he grew tired.

"'Ho!' he said to himself, 'I am far enough now and I shall sleep. It's easy to steal from the Sun – just as easy as stealing from the Bear or the Beaver.'

"He folded the leggings and put them under his head as the Sun had done, and went to sleep. He had a dream and it waked him with a start. Bad deeds bring bad dreams to us all. *Old-*man sat up and there was the Sun looking right in his face and laughing. He was frightened and ran away, leaving the leggings behind him.

"Laughingly, the Sun put on the leggings and went on toward the west, for he is always busy. He thought he would see *Old-*man no more, but it takes more than one lesson to teach a fool to be wise, and *Old-*man hid in the timber until the Sun had traveled out of sight. Then he ran westward and hid himself near the Sun's lodge again, intending to wait for the night and steal the leggings a second time.

"He was much afraid this time, but as soon as the Sun was asleep he crept to the lodge and peeked inside. Here he stopped and looked about, for he was afraid the Sun would hear his heart beating. Finally he started toward the Sun's bed and just then a great white Owl flew from off the lodge poles, and this scared him more, for that is very bad luck and he knew it; but he kept on creeping until he could almost touch the Sun."

"All about the lodge were beautiful linings, tanned and painted by the Moon, and the queer signs on them made the old coward tremble. He heard a night-bird call outside and he thought it would surely wake the Sun; so he hastened to the bed and, with cunning fingers, stole the leggings, as he had done the night before, without waking the great sleeper. Then he crept out of the lodge, talking bravely to himself as cowards do when they are afraid.

"'Now,' he said to himself, 'I shall run faster and farther than before. I shall not stop running while the night lasts, and I shall stay in the mountains all the time when the Sun is at work in the daytime!'

"Away he went – running as the Buffalo runs – straight ahead, looking at nothing, hearing nothing, stopping at nothing. When day began to break *Old*-man was far from the Sun's lodge and he hid himself in a deep gulch among some bushes that grew there. He listened a long time before he dared to go to sleep, but finally he did. He was tired from his great run and slept soundly and for a long time, but when he opened his eyes – there was the Sun looking straight at him, and this time he was scowling. *Old*-man started to run away but the Sun grabbed him and threw him down upon his back. My! but the Sun was angry, and he said:

"'*Old*-man, *you* are a clever thief but a mighty fool as well, for you steal from me and expect to hide away. Twice you have stolen the leggings my wife made for me, and twice I have found you easily. Don't you know that the whole world is my lodge and that you can never get outside of it, if you run your foolish legs off? Don't you know that I light all of my lodge every day and search it carefully? Don't you know that nothing can hide from me and live? I shall not harm you this time, but I warn you now, that if you ever steal from me again, I will hurt you badly. Now go, and don't let me catch you stealing again!'

"Away went *Old*-man, and on toward the west went the busy Sun. That is all.

"Now go to bed; for I would talk of other things with my friend, who knows of war as I do. Ho!"

# WHY THE NIGHT-HAWK'S WINGS
## ARE BEAUTIFUL

# WHY THE NIGHT-HAWK'S WINGS
## ARE BEAUTIFUL

I WAS awakened by the voice of the camp-crier, and although it was yet dark I listened his message.

The camp was to move. All were to go to the mouth of the Maria's – "The River That Scolds at the Other" – the Indians call this stream, that disturbs the waters of the Missouri with its swifter flood.

On through the camp the crier rode, and behind him the lodge-fires glowed in answer to his call. The village was awake, and soon the thunder of hundreds of hoofs told me that the pony-bands were being driven into camp, where the faithful were being roped for the journey. Fires flickered in the now fading darkness, and down came the lodges as though wizard hands had touched them. Before the sun had come to light the world, we were on our way to "The River That Scolds at the Other."

Not a cloud was in the sky, and the wind was still. The sun came and touched the plains and hilltops with the light that makes all wild things glad. Here and there a jackrabbit scurried away, often followed by a pack of dogs, and sometimes, though not often, they were over-taken and devoured on the spot. Bands of graceful an-

73

telope bounded out of our way, stopping on a knoll to watch the strange procession with wondering eyes, and once we saw a dust-cloud raised by a moving herd of buffalo, in the distance.

So the day wore on, the scene constantly changing as we traveled. Wolves and coyotes looked at us from almost every knoll and hilltop; and sage-hens sneaked to cover among the patches of sage-brush, scarcely ten feet away from our ponies. Toward sundown we reached a grove of cottonwoods near the mouth of the Maria's, and in an incredibly short space of time the lodges took form. Soon, from out the tops of a hundred camps, smoke was curling just as though the lodges had been there always, and would forever remain.

As soon as supper was over, I found the children, and together we sought War Eagle's lodge. He was in a happy mood and insisted upon smoking two pipes before commencing his storytelling. At last he said:

"Tonight I shall tell you why the Night-hawk wears fine clothes. My grandfather told me about it when I was young. I am sure you have seen the Night-hawk sailing over you, dipping and making that strange noise. Of course, there is a reason for it.

"*Old*-man was traveling one day in the springtime; but the weather was fine for that time of year. He stopped often and spoke to the bird-people and to the animal-people, for he was in good humor that day. He talked pleasantly with the trees, and his heart grew ten-

74

der. That is, he had good thoughts; and of course they made him happy. Finally he felt tired and sat down to rest on a big, round stone – the kind of stone our white friend there calls a bowlder. Here he rested for a while, but the stone was cold, and he felt it through his robe; so he said:

"'Stone, you seem cold today. You may have my robe. I have hundreds of robes in my camp, and I don't need this one at all.' That was a lie he told about having so many robes. All he had was the one he wore.

"He spread his robe over the stone, and then started down the hill, naked, for it was really a fine day. But storms hide in the mountains, and are never far away when it is springtime. Soon it began to snow – then the wind blew from the north with a good strength behind it. *Old*-man said:

"'Well, I guess I do need that robe myself, after all. That stone never did anything for me anyhow. Nobody is ever good to a stone. I'll just go back and get my robe.'

"Back he went and found the stone. Then he pulled the robe away, and wrapped it about himself. Ho! but that made the stone angry – Ho! *Old*-man started to run down the hill, and the stone ran after him. Ho! it was a funny race they made, over the grass, over smaller stones, and over logs that lay in the way, but *Old*-man managed to keep ahead until he stubbed his toe on a big sagebrush, and fell – swow!

"'Now I have you!' cried the stone – 'now I'll kill you, too! Now I will teach you to give presents and then take them away,' and the stone rolled right on top of *Old*-man, and sat on his back.

"It was a big stone, you see, and *Old*-man couldn't move it at all. He tried to throw off the stone but failed. He squirmed and twisted – no use – the stone held him fast. He called the stone some names that are not good; but that never helps any. At last he began to call:

"'Help! – Help! – Help!' but nobody heard him except the Night-hawk, and he told the *Old*-man that he would help him all he could; so he flew away up in the air – so far that he looked like a black speck. Then he came down straight and struck that rock an awful blow – 'swow!' – and broke it in two pieces. Indeed he did. The blow was so great that it spoiled the Night-hawk's bill, forever – made it queer in shape, and jammed his head, so that it is queer, too. But he broke the rock, and *Old*-man stood upon his feet.

"'Thank you, Brother Night-hawk,' said *Old*-man, 'now I will do something for you. I am going to make you different from other birds – make you so people will always notice you.

"You know that when you break a rock the powdered stone is white, like snow; and there is always some of the white powder whenever you break a rock, by pounding it. Well, *Old*-man took some of the fine powdered stone and shook it on the Night-hawk's wings

76

in spots and stripes – made the great white stripes you have seen on his wings, and told him that no other bird could have such marks on his clothes.

"All the Night-hawk's children dress the same way now; and they always will as long as there are Night-hawks. Of course, their clothes make them proud; and that is why they keep flying over people's heads – soaring and dipping and turning all the time, to show off their pretty wings.

"That is all for tonight. Muskrat, tell your father I would run Buffalo with him tomorrow – Ho!"

# THE FIRE-LEGGINGS

## THE FIRE-LEGGINGS

THERE had been a sudden change in the weather. A cold rain was falling, and the night comes early when the clouds hang low. The children loved a bright fire, and tonight War Eagle's lodge was light as day. Away off on the plains a wolf was howling, and the rain pattered upon the lodge as though it never intended to quit. It was a splendid night for storytelling, and War Eagle filled and lighted the great stone pipe, while the children made themselves comfortable about the fire.

A spark sprang from the burning sticks, and fell upon Fine Bow's bare leg. They all laughed heartily at the boy's antics to rid himself of the burning coal; and as soon as the laughing ceased War Eagle laid aside the pipe. An Indian's pipe is large to look at, but holds little tobacco.

"See your shadows on the lodge wall?" asked the old warrior. The children said they saw them, and he continued:

"Some day I will tell you a story about them, and how they drew the arrows of our enemies, but tonight I am going to tell you of the great fire-leggings.

"It was long before there were men and women on

the world, but my grandfather told me what I shall now tell you.

"The gray light that hides the night-stars was creeping through the forests, and the wind the Sun sends to warn the people of his coming was among the fir tops. Flowers, on slender stems, bent their heads out of respect for the herald-wind's Master, and from the dead top of a pine-tree the Yellowhammer beat upon his drum and called the Sun is awake – all hail the Sun!'

"Then the bush-birds began to sing the song of the morning, and from alders the Robins joined, until all live things were awakened by the great music. Where the tall ferns grew, the Doe waked her Fawns, and taught them to do homage to the Great Light. In the creeks, where the water was still and clear, and where throughout the day, like a delicate damaskeen, the shadows of leaves that overhang would lie, the Speckled Trout broke the surface of the pool in his gladness of the coming day. Pine-squirrels chattered gaily, and loudly proclaimed what the wind had told; and all the shadows were preparing for a great journey to the Sand Hills, where the ghost-people dwell.

"Under a great spruce-tree – where the ground was soft and dry, *Old*-man slept. The joy that thrilled creation disturbed him not, although the Sun was near. The bird-people looked at the sleeper in wonder, but the Pine-squirrel climbed the great spruce-tree with a pine-cone in his mouth. Quickly he ran out on the limb that spread over *Old*-man, and dropped the cone on the sleeper's face. Then he scolded *Old*-man, saying: 'Get up – get up – lazy one – lazy one – get up – get up.'

"Rubbing his eyes in anger, *Old*-man sat up and saw the Sun coming – his hunting leggings slipping through the thickets – setting them afire, till all the Deer and Elk ran out and sought new places to hide.

"'Ho, Sun!' called *Old*-man, 'those are mighty leggings you wear. No wonder you are a great hunter. Your leggings set fire to all the thickets, and by the light you can easily see the Deer and Elk; they cannot hide. Ho! Give them to me and I shall then be the great hunter and never be hungry.'

"'Good,' said the Sun, 'take them, and let me see you wear my leggings.'

"*Old*-man was glad in his heart, for he was lazy, and now he thought he could kill the game without much work, and that he could be a great hunter – as great as the Sun. He put on the leggings and at once began to hunt the thickets, for he was hungry. Very soon the leggings began to burn his legs. The faster he traveled the hotter they grew, until in pain he cried out to the Sun to come and take back his leggings; but the Sun would not hear him. On and on *Old*-man ran. Faster and faster he flew through the country, setting fire to the brush and grass as he passed. Finally he came to a great river, and jumped in. Sizzzzzzz – the water said, when *Old*-

man's legs touched it. It cried out, as it does when it is sprinkled upon hot stones in the sweat-lodge, for the leggings were very hot. But standing in the cool water, *Old*-man took off the leggings and threw them out upon the shore, where the Sun found them later in the day.

"The Sun's clothes were too big for *Old*-man, and his work too great.

"We should never ask to do the things which Manitou did not intend us to do. If we keep this always in mind we shall never get into trouble.

"Be yourselves always. That is what Manitou intended. Never blame the Wolf for what he does. He was made to do such things. Now I want you to go to your fathers' lodges and sleep. Tomorrow night I will tell you why there are so many snakes in the world. Ho!"

# WHY THE INDIANS WHIP THE
# BUFFALO-BERRIES FROM THE BUSHES

## Why the Indians Whip the
## Buffalo-Berries from the Bushes

THE Indian believes that all things live again; that all were created by one and the same power; that nothing was created in vain; and that in the life beyond the grave he will know all things that he knew here. In that other world, he expects to make his living easier, and not suffer from hunger or cold; therefore, all things that die must go to his heaven, in order that he may be supplied with the necessities of life.

The sun is not the Indian's God, but a personification of the Deity; His greatest manifestation; His light.

The Indian believes that to each of His creations God gave some peculiar power, and that the possessors of these special favors are His lieutenants and keepers of the several special attributes; such as wisdom, cunning, speed, and the knowledge of healing wounds. These wonderful gifts, he knew, were bestowed as favors by a common God, and therefore he revered these powers, and, without jealousy, paid tribute thereto.

The bear was great in war, because before the horse came, he would sometimes charge the camps and kill or wound many people. Although many arrows were sent into his huge carcass, he seldom died. Hence the

Indian was sure that the bear could heal his wounds. That the bear possessed a great knowledge of roots and berries, the Indian knew, for he often saw him digging the one and stripping the others from the bushes. The buffalo, the beaver, the wolf, and the eagle – each possessed strange powers that commanded the Indian's admiration and respect, as did many other things in creation.

If about to go to war, the Indian did not ask his God for aid – oh, no. He realized that God made his enemy, too; and that if He desired that enemy's destruction, it would be accomplished without man's aid. So the Indian sang his song to the bear, prayed to the bear, and thus invoked aid from a brute, and not his God, when he sought to destroy his fellows.

Whenever the Indian addressed the Great God, his prayer was for life, and life alone. He is the most religious man I have ever known, as well as the most superstitious; and there are stories dealing with his religious faith that are startling, indeed.

"It is the wrong time of year to talk about berries," said War Eagle, that night in the lodge, "but I shall tell you why your mothers whip the buffalo-berries from the bushes. *Old*-man was the one who started it, and our people have followed his example ever since. Ho! *Old*-man made a fool of himself that day.

"It was the time when buffalo-berries are red and ripe. All of the bushes along the rivers were loaded with them, and our people were about to gather what

88

they needed, when *Old*-man changed things, as far as the gathering was concerned.

"He was traveling along a river, and hungry, as he always was. Standing on the bank of that river, he saw great clusters of red, ripe buffalo-berries in the water. They were larger than any berries he had ever seen, and he said:

"'I guess I will get those berries. They look fine, and I need them. Besides, some of the people will see them and get them, if I don't.'

"He jumped into the water; looked for the berries; but they were not there. For a time, *Old*-man stood in the river and looked for the berries, but they were gone.

"After a while he climbed out on the bank again, and when the water got smooth once more there were the berries – the same berries, in the same spot in the water.

"'Ho! – that is a funny thing. I wonder where they hid that time. I must have those berries!' he said to himself.

"In he went again – splashing the water like a Grizzly Bear. He looked about him and the berries were gone again. The water was rippling about him, but there were no berries at all. He felt on the bottom of the river but they were not there.

"'Well,' he said, 'I will climb out and watch to see where they come from; then I shall grab them when I hit the water next time.'

"He did that; but he couldn't tell where the berries

came from. As soon as the water settled and became smooth – there were the berries – the same as before. Ho! – *Old*-man was wild; he was angry, I tell you. And in he went flat on his stomach! He made an awful splash and mussed the water greatly; but there were no berries.

"'I know what I shall do. I will stay right here and wait for those berries; that is what I shall do'; and he did.

"He thought maybe somebody was looking at him and would laugh, so he glanced along the bank. And there, right over the water, he saw the same bunch of berries on some tall bushes. Don't you see? *Old*-man saw the shadow of the berry-bunch; not the berries. He saw the red shadow-berries on the water; that was all, and he was such a fool he didn't know they were not real.

"Well, now he was angry in truth. Now he was ready for war. He climbed out on the bank again and cut a club. Then he went at the buffalo-berry bushes and pounded them till all of the red berries fell upon the ground – till the branches were bare of berries.

"'There,' he said, 'that's what you get for making a fool of the man who made you. You shall be beaten every year as long as you live, to pay for what you have done; you and your children, too.'

"That is how it all came about, and that is why your mothers whip the buffalo-berry bushes and then pick the berries from the ground. Ho!"

# WHY THE BIRCH-TREE WEARS THE SLASHES IN ITS BARK

## Why the Birch-Tree Wears the Slashes in Its Bark

THE white man has never understood the Indian, and the example set the Western tribes of the plains by our white brethren has not been such as to inspire the red man with either confidence or respect for our laws or our religion. The fighting trapper, the border bandit, the horse-thief and rustler, in whose stomach legitimately acquired beef would cause colic – were the Indians' first acquaintances who wore a white skin, and he did not know that they were not of the best type. Being outlaws in every sense, these men sought shelter from the Indian in the wilderness; and he learned of their ways about his lodge-fire, or in battle, often provoked by the white ruffian in the hope of gain. They lied to the Indian – these first white acquaintances, and in after-years, the great Government of the United States lied and lied again, until he has come to believe that there is no truth in the white man's heart. And I don't blame him.

The Indian is a charitable man. I don't believe he ever refused food and shelter or abused a visitor. He has never been a bigot, and concedes to every other man the right to his own beliefs. Further than that, the Indian believes that every man's religion and belief is right and proper for that man's self.

It was blowing a gale and snow was being driven in fine flakes across the plains when we went to the lodge for a story. Every minute the weather was growing colder, and an early fall storm of severity was upon us. The wind seemed to add to the good nature of our host as he filled and passed me the pipe.

"This is the night I was to tell you about the Birch-Tree, and the wind will help to make you understand," said War Eagle after we had finished smoking.

"Of course," he continued, "this all happened in the summer-time when the weather was warm, very warm. Sometimes, you know, there are great winds in the summer, too.

"It was a hot day, and *Old*-man was trying to sleep, but the heat made him sick. He wandered to a hilltop for air; but there was no air. Then he went down to the river and found no relief. He traveled to the timberlands, and there the heat was great, although he found plenty of shade. The traveling made him warmer, of course, but he wouldn't stay still.

"By and by he called to the winds to blow, and they commenced. First they didn't blow very hard, because they were afraid they might make *Old*-man angry, but he kept crying:

"Blow harder – harder – harder! Blow worse than

94

ever you blew before, and send this heat away from the world.'

"So, of course, the winds did blow harder – harder than they ever had blown before."

"'Bend and break, Fir-Tree!' cried *Old*-man, and the Fir-Tree did bend and break. 'Bend and break, Pine-Tree!' and the Pine-Tree did bend and break. 'Bend and break, Spruce Tree!' and the Spruce-Tree did bend and break. 'Bend and break, O Birch-Tree!' and the Birch-Tree did bend, but it wouldn't break – no, sir! – it wouldn't break!

"'Ho! Birch-Tree, won't you mind me? Bend and break! I tell you,' but all the Birch-Tree would do was to bend.

"It bent to the ground; it bent double to please *Old*-man, but it would not break.

"'Blow harder, wind!' cried *Old*-man, 'blow harder and break the Birch-Tree.' The wind tried to blow harder, but it couldn't, and that made the thing worse, because *Old*-man was so angry he went crazy. 'Break! I tell you – break!' screamed *Old*-man to the Birch-Tree.

"'I won't break,' replied the Birch; 'I shall never break for any wind. I will bend, but I shall never, never break.'

"'You won't, hey?' cried *Old*-man, and he rushed at the Birch-Tree with his hunting-knife. He grabbed the top of the Birch because it was touching the ground, and began slashing the bark of the Birch-Tree with the knife. All up and down the trunk of the tree *Old*-man slashed, until the Birch was covered with the knife slashes.

"'There! that is for not minding me. That will do you good! As long as time lasts you shall always look like that, Birch-Tree; always be marked as one who will not mind its maker. Yes, and all the Birch-Trees in the world shall have the same marks forever.' They do, too. You have seen them and have wondered why the Birch-Tree is so queerly marked. Now you know.'

"That is all – Ho!"